PICTORIAL SUPPLEMENT

TO LMS LOCOMOTIVE PROFILE No. 15
THE 'ROYAL SCOTS'

by
JOHN JENNISON & DAVID HUNT

No. 46112 Sherwood Forester passing Whitehall Junction leaving Leeds with the Down Thames-Clyde Express. The Holbeck rebuilt 'Scots' did some of the finest work ever seen in steam days over the Leeds – Settle – Carlisle line with such trains as this but except for the five at the Leeds shed no more were allocated to the Midland Division until 1957. KENNETH FIELD/RAIL ARCHIVE STEPHENSON

WILD SWAN BOOKS

FOREWORD

As regular readers of our works will be aware, the concept of pictorial supplements to the *LMS Locomotive Profile* series began with No. 5 on the early mixed traffic Class 5s, the aim being to make available more good quality photographs than we had room for in the main title itself. This has proved to be a popular move and the supplements have been well received but as we have tried to do with the *Profiles*, we have taken note of readers' suggestions with the result that the contents of this volume are somewhat different from before. Some readers have commented that the *Pictorial Supplements* should be just what their title suggests – supplementary to the *Profiles* and almost purely pictorial in nature. As with the *Pictorial Supplements* for the 'Coronations' and 'Princess Royals' we have taken into account readers' suggestions and therefore have not summarised the information contained in the main title but have simply provided short lead-ins to each section, all of which contain detailed photograph captions. This approach suits us as it means that more space is then available for the pictorial content and it enables us to include several drawings that we have been given since the *Profile* was published.

Also, in keeping with requests from readers, we have included as many pictures as possible of the engines doing what they were built for, i.e., hauling trains. We have arranged them in chronological order to cover the whole period from early LMS days until withdrawal by British Railways and have grouped them geographically within each section.

In a slight departure from previous *Pictorial Supplements* and in order to take advantage of the quality of the pictures we have selected from Rail-Online and Rail Archive Stephenson, around half of the book consists of full-page photographs. Overall, we hope that the selected views have resulted in a mix which illustrates the Class over the four decades that the engines were in service. Note that, as with the *Profile*, we will not be dealing with 6399 *Fury*/6170 *British Legion* because it was significantly different from the rest of the Class and in our view merits separate coverage.

Once again, we would welcome comments, amendments and suggestions that should be sent to the editor responsible for both the *Profiles* and *Supplements*, David Hunt, through our link on the LMS Society website at www.lmssociety.org.uk or by post via Wild Swan Books.

Since writing this book we have lost one of the *LMS Profiles* team members, namely Bob Essery who died in November 2021. Bob was without doubt one of the best known and most prolific authors of and contributors to a wide variety of railway and railway modelling titles and articles and was the prime mover in establishing the *LMS Locomotive Profiles* series. His chief contribution to the books was in providing illustrations from his extensive photograph collection as well as carrying out some of the research effort that has gone into their production, and reading through the manuscripts prior to publication to enhance them with the benefit of his own wide experience. As well as being a colleague of the production team, though, he was a good friend and will be sorely missed.

Throughout this book, left-hand and right-hand invariably refer to those sides of the locomotive or tender when looking towards the front. This applies despite the orientation of photographs. Where dates of conversion and other modifications are given these refer to when the engines left the works and re-entered traffic.

Front cover photographs:
A taper boiler and a parallel boiler 'Royal Scot' rest side by side after arrival at Euston. Bushbury's 46110 Grenadier Guardsman *is on the right and Edge Hill's 46135* The East Lancashire Regiment *on the left. This picture was taken after November 1950 when 46135 was fitted with smoke deflectors and before July 1951 when 46110 was transferred away from Bushbury to Carlisle Upperby;* Grenadier Guardsman *was itself rebuilt with a taper boiler in January 1953.*
W.J.V. ANDERSON/RAIL ARCHIVE STEPHENSON

No. 46156 The South Wales Borderer *in British Railways lined black with Gill Sans smokebox door numberplate and cabside numerals and 8¾in BRITISH RAILWAYS lettering on the tender. It had been renumbered in February 1949 and was rebuilt with a taper boiler in 1954.* WWW.RAIL-ONLINE.CO.UK

© Wild Swan Books Ltd. and the authors 2022
ISBN 978 1 912038 66 4

WILD SWAN BOOKS LTD.

Designed by Stephen Phillips. Printed by Lavenham Press, Suffolk.

Published by
WILD SWAN BOOKS LTD.
4 Tollbridge Studios, Toll Bridge Road, Bath BA1 7DE

THE 'ROYAL SCOTS'

INTRODUCTION AND ORIGINS

When they appeared in 1927, the 'Royal Scots' were the first LMS express passenger design and until the arrival of the production series of 'Princess Royals' in 1935 and then the 'Coronations' from 1937, the 'Royal Scots' held sway on the principal Western and Northern Division expresses. They were introduced in a hurry, with the first fifty entering service within less than a year after they were authorised, because the LMS urgently needed a large express engine for its West Coast Main Line.

During preparation of the *Profile* we tried to provide a full and balanced account of the gestation of the Class which in some areas contradicts what had been written before, much of the latter having passed into folklore and become the generally perceived wisdom. These differences have, of course, been carried over to this volume and as with our previous efforts, we have tried to make a clear distinction between unequivocal statements based on primary evidence, reasonable estimates arrived at by analysis of available data, and instances where we have had to rely on secondary sources. Where we give dates or details without reserve, it means that we are confident of our facts whereas when there is any doubt we state as such.

The urgent need for an express passenger locomotive led to the 'Royal Scots' being designed by a combination of the Locomotive Design Office at Derby and the North British Locomotive Company drawing office at Springburn, the latter being responsible for the detailed design. The boiler was a development of those used on the Compound 4-4-0s, the outside motion and valves were based on those used in the 2-6-4 tanks and other standard Derby features were incorporated including the 'Old Standard' 3,500 gallon tender.

Although the engines were initially successful, a number of problems emerged during their first few years in service. Probably the most the significant was the dramatic increase in coal consumption due to steam leakage from the single, broad, cast-iron Schmidt piston valve rings; these were replaced from late 1929 by the multiple, narrow ring type. After a serious accident in 1931, smoke deflectors were fitted from early 1932 and the Midland Railway pattern bogies were replaced by GWR type side bolster bogies from 1934 to improve the riding at high speed.

The most significant change came during World War 2 when 6103 and 6109 were rebuilt with 2A taper boilers in 1943 following the successful application of these to two 'Jubilees' in the previous year. At the same time, they were given new cylinders and new design smoke boxes to overcome the problem with the original built-up smokeboxes that were difficult to keep airtight. The remainder of the class were similarly converted although the process was protracted and was not completed until 1955.

Nos. 6141 and 6142, both yet to be named, soon after delivery to Crewe from the North British Locomotive Company at Glasgow in October 1927. The LMS wanted the first engine to be delivered within twenty-five weeks from placing the order with NBL. The rate of work to achieve this was intense and to minimise production time, twenty-five were built to NBL Order No. L833 at Queen's Park Works and numbered 6100-6124 whilst 6125-6149 were turned out from Hyde Park Works to Order L834. Delivery of the last locomotive was on 15th November 1927 when 6149 left Hyde Park Works but it wasn't recorded as being accepted into LMS stock until 4th December.
W.H. WHITWORTH/RAIL ARCHIVE STEPHENSON

No. 6124, yet to be named London Scottish, passing Oxenholme in May 1928 with the 10.35am Euston to Carlisle express consisting of a very mixed bag of coaching stock typical of the period. 6124 had a white enamelled Western Division shed code plate bearing the number 15 for Crewe North.
F.R. HEBRON/RAIL ARCHIVE STEPHENSON

THE 'ROYAL SCOTS'

One of the drawbacks of the large diameter smokebox and short chimney on the 'Royal Scots', particularly when they were driven with a short cut-off, was that smoke and vapour from the chimney often failed to clear the low-pressure zone that formed around the boiler and tended to cling to the barrel. This obscured the driver's view and by 1929 complaints about the 'Scots' were sufficiently numerous for experiments to be initiated with various modifications to the front ends of several engines including 6100 Royal Scot. The simple shovel rim smoke deflector it had when leaving Carlisle in 1929 with the 11am Liverpool express did not prove effective and side plates were fitted to all of the Class in 1932. Two additional dogs had been added at the lower part of the smokebox door in an attempt to maintain an air tight seal.   F.R. HEBRON/RAIL ARCHIVE STEPHENSON

No. 6110 Grenadier Guardsman *leaving Rugby with the down Mid-day Scot in around 1930. As soon as they entered service the 'Scots' took over all of the principal Western Division expresses such as 'The Mid-day'. The LMS standard livery was changed in December 1927; the paint scheme was retained but the stock numbers replaced the roundel on the cab sides and LMS lettering was applied to the tender.* T.G. HEPBURN/RAIL ARCHIVE STEPHENSON

No. 6129 Comet *waiting at Willesden Junction Low Level station in around 1930. It became* The Scottish Horse *at the end of 1935 and the* Comet *name was re-used on a 'Jubilee'.* J.N. HALL/RAIL ARCHIVE STEPHENSON

DETAILS

The large diameter smokebox and short chimney of the parallel boiler engines soon led to complaints from drivers that smoke and vapour from the chimney was drifting downwards and obscuring their view ahead. Experiments with a variety of devices were made between 1929 and 1930 and after a serious high-speed derailment of 6114 at Leighton Buzzard in March 1931 was partially attributed to this problem, smoke deflector plates were tested on three engines and these were quickly fitted to all of the class from early 1932.

In an attempt to improve riding at high speed, new bogies of the bolster bearing type that was standard at Swindon were fitted from 1934, although they retained the wheels, axles, axleboxes and frame stays of the originals. Other modifications introduced after William Stanier arrived from the GWR were the removal of the crosshead-driven vacuum pumps and bogie brakes, and fitting of various types of speed recorders.

Although additional coal rails had been added to the 'Old standard' 3,500 gallon tenders between 1931 and 1933 to increase their effective coal capacity, these were replaced in the end of 1935 by the standard Stanier 9 ton 4,500 gallon type, which remained with the Class until withdrawal.

When the 'Scots' were rebuilt with 2A taper boilers between 1943 and 1955, they retained their original cabs, wheels, motion, bogies, brake and sanding gear. Initially they did not have smoke deflectors, but these were added from 1947 onwards following problems with smoke drifting from the relatively soft exhaust created by their new double chimneys.

Under BR, rebuilding continued until the final example 46137 was converted in 1955. The final modifications were BR speed indicators and AWS that were fitted to all except a handful of engines between 1959 and 1962.

As would be expected of a principal passenger class, new liveries were quickly applied to the 'Royal Scots' so they went through a cycle starting with LMS crimson lake, followed by LMS black, BR black and finally BR green. Insignia also changed and produced many permutations that we have attempted to summarise in the *Profile*.

When the first fifty 'Scots' were built, the LMS passenger engine livery as shown by 6100 Royal Scot in 1928 was basically that of the Midland Railway post-1906 crimson lake with a few minor differences. The lining colour is usually just described as yellow but at that time was almost certainly the same pale straw that was used by the Midland in its later years. The Company emblems on the cab sides were the 14in diameter 'button' transfers, tender side numerals were scroll and serif gold, shaded black to the right and below and 18in high not including the shading, which was 7/8in wide. Between the gold and black was a fine 1/8in white line. Smokebox door numberplate and power classification figures were also scroll and serif, the latter being simply 6. W.H. WHITWORTH/RAIL ARCHIVE STEPHENSON

No. 6125, yet to be named Lancashire Witch, *at Camden shed when new in 1927. This was the first of the twenty-five engines built at NBL's Hyde Park Works, all of which were originally named after historic locomotives ranging from those performing in the Rainhill Trials, through the early days of pre-Grouping LMS companies' constituents to more recent L&NWR examples. The other twenty-five engines, built at the NBL Queen's Park Works, had a mixture of Scottish names and regimental personnel of the British Army. The maker's plate on 6125 is circular whereas those on 6100-24 were diamond-shaped. The bogie brakes and crosshead vacuum pumps were removed from the Class after William Stanier arrived on the LMS in 1932.*
W.J. REYNOLDS/RAIL ARCHIVE STEPHENSON

Brand new 6153, with backing plates ready for its The Royal Dragoon *nameplates to be fitted, at Derby shed in July 1930 was one of the final twenty engines built at Derby in 1930. These incorporated a number of modifications to the original design, the most important of which was the use of multiple, rather than single, piston valve rings. Externally, there were two additional dogs at the bottom of the smokebox door and additional coal rails on the tender which increased the notional capacity from the 5½ tons which had proved inadequate on long through runs. The power class was by then 6P rather than the original plain 6.*
W.H. WHITWORTH/RAIL ARCHIVE STEPHENSON

THE 'ROYAL SCOTS'

No. 6161 King's Own *when fitted with one of the various experimental smoke deflecting arrangements applied to several of the class starting in 1929. None of these proved effective and the familiar smoke deflector plates were adopted in 1931 and fitted to all of the engines by early 1932.*
C.R. GORDON STUART/RAIL ARCHIVE STEPHENSON

The first type of smoke deflectors, otherwise 'downdraught plates' or 'blinker plates' as they were called in some LMS documents, fitted in 1931 and 1932 were as illustrated in this picture of 6156 The South Wales Borderer *at Polmadie in around 1934. As can be seen, they were flat, as was the beading round the edge, whilst the commode handrails remained in their original position above the front footsteps on the footplate.*
RAIL ARCHIVE STEPHENSON

No. 6109 Royal Engineer at Crewe in 1938 had the short-lived 1936 livery with sans serif numerals and letters. It was paired with a Stanier 4,000 gallon riveted tender in April 1936. Although its crosshead pump was still in place, there were numerous other detail changes since the engine left the Queens Park Works of NBL in September 1927. Its smokebox door had been fitted with an extra two dogs, it had acquired a new side bolster bogie without brakes, the split brasses at the fronts of the coupling rods had been replaced by solid bushes, the corners of the footsteps had been turned up, side screens had been fitted to the cab, rain gutters added to the eaves and the small upper front windows had been removed and the apertures filled in. The pattern of smoke deflectors went through several iterations. At first the plates were flat, but then the top portions of the plates were bent over slightly to improve the smoke lifting qualities. When photographed 6109 had two-piece plates with a horizontal joint at the main platform level, butt strips inside and snap-head rivets. WWW.RAIL-ONLINE.CO.UK

No. 6107 Argyll and Sutherland Highlander at Crewe in 1936 soon after it received a Stanier 4,000 gallon tender with riveted tanks which had been built for 'Jubilee' 5573. It had the final arrangement of smoke deflectors which lasted until the locomotives were rebuilt. The main portions of the deflector plates were moved further out from the smokebox, still with a gentle curve to the top, but the lower part in front of the platform drop section remained where it had been so that there was a sideways step between the upper and lower plates, and the commode handles were moved to the lower plate. No. 6107 had a side bolster bogie without brakes, the crosshead vacuum pump had been removed, the split brasses at the fronts of the coupling rods replaced by solid bushes, the corners of the footsteps turned up, side screens fitted to the cab, and rain gutters added to the eaves. WWW.RAIL-ONLINE.CO.UK

THE 'ROYAL SCOTS'

The tender of 6134 Honourable Artillery Company *was being filled to the limit with coal at Polmadie shed in around 1947. It was one of only a handful of parallel boiler engines repainted in the LMS 1946 lined-black express passenger livery. The lining was pale straw and maroon, the straw colour being paler than that used previously and more like an off-white whilst the maroon was much darker than crimson lake. The hand painted cabside numerals were 12in sans serif in pale straw with inset maroon lining and were positioned in line with the 14in pale straw, sans serif tender letters; the 6P power classification was below the numbers.*

RAIL ARCHIVE STEPHENSON

Another parallel boiler engine repainted in LMS 1946 livery was 46110 Grenadier Guardsman *photographed waiting at Crewe in 1949. It displays one of the hybrid livery combinations common in the first few years after nationalisation, retaining the basic LMS livery with new BR numbers using a Gill Sans smokebox plate and Gill Sans 8in cab numbers that were applied in w/e 2nd April 1949.*

RAIL ARCHIVE STEPHENSON

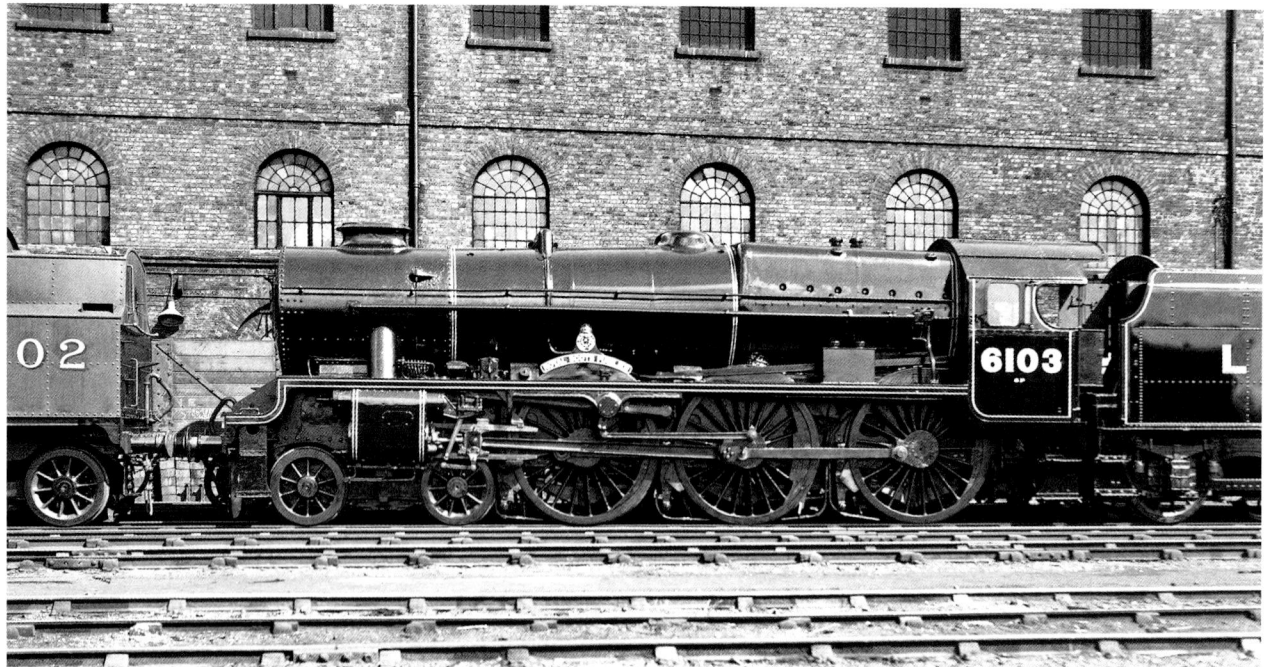

The first of the Class to be converted with a taper boiler was 6103 Royal Scots Fusilier *in June 1943. In this picture, its original wartime unlined black had just been replaced by 1946 lined black livery during a Heavy General repair at Crewe completed in September 1947. Other changes since it was rebuilt include the characteristic rear sandbox above the footplate alongside the firebox, which was fitted in June 1945, and plain in place of fluted coupling rods.*

J.N. HALL/RAIL ARCHIVE STEPHENSON

No. 46166 London Rifle Brigade *shows another example of the early BR hybrid liveries. It had been converted in January 1945, repainted in 1946 livery in October 1947 and was renumbered in July 1948 still in 1946 livery using block style 10in cab numbers while retaining the LMS tender lettering.*

WWW.RAIL-ONLINE.CO.UK

THE 'ROYAL SCOTS'

13

This close-up picture of 46111 Royal Fusilier *after arrival at Euston in the early 1960s shows many features of the taper boiler engines. It had a double chimney and smoke deflectors with overhead electrification warning plates and has Stanier bevel-rimmed bogie wheels combined with original pattern coupled wheels. It has the later type of top feed casing which was fitted on the first barrel ring with two washout plugs at the front of the barrel. The coupling rods were fluted, there was a small oilbox on top of the crossheads to lubricate the connecting rod little end with a separate oil box for the lower slide bar on the front of the crosshead between the piston rod and the lower flange. On the platform were the fillers for the sandboxes for the leading and middle coupled wheels which had lids with concave tops and integrally cast handles, and the Silvertown mechanical lubricator which pressure fed oil to the piston and valve spindle glands. The brakes were operated from a steam cylinder inside the frames under the drag box which drove a crank that acted on transverse beams between the bottom ends of the brake hangers which carried the brake blocks in front of the coupled wheels. The cylinders had three drain cocks with horizontal poppet valves operated by a linkage from the cab and short copper drain pipes clipped together at the front. No. 46111 had the later type of Turton & Platt 'No-weld' type buffers with footsteps on top of the buffer casings. WWW.RAIL-ONLINE.CO.UK*

The smoke deflectors on 46106 Gordon Highlander were replaced in May 1954 with a type similar to those on the BR 'Britannias'. Although these were an improvement on those fitted to the taper boiler engines, 46106 remained the only example, retaining the later deflectors until withdrawal in 1962. Note that unlike the normal pattern, there was edge beading on the outside only, there was no attachment to the boiler handrails, the commode handles were mounted on the sides of the deflectors and there were handrails on the plates themselves. No. 46106 had Stanier-pattern bogie wheels, footsteps with fully turned-up ends, and Turton & Platt 'No-weld' buffer casings. It was fitted with AWS in October 1959; the receiver was mounted on the front bogie stretcher whilst a protector plate was attached to the buffer beam to prevent damage from a swinging front coupling.

WWW.RAIL-ONLINE.CO.UK

THE 'ROYAL SCOTS'

No. 6111 Royal Fusilier with an Up express at Crewe in the early 1930s still had its original 'Old Standard' tender, which was essentially the same as the Midland Railway Deeley tenders dating from 1905. It soon became apparent that coal consumption of a 'Scot' on a non-stop Euston to Carlisle run could be anything from 5¼ to 6 tons, which for a tender that could carry a notional 5½ tons was too close for any sort of comfort, even if the coal was piled as high as possible. Before being fitted with additional coal rails, tenders were sometimes carefully stacked with large slabs of coal arranged to form makeshift extensions of the sides so that enough could be carried but this took a long time as well as being somewhat unstable after the first few tons were used. The last twenty of the Class had tenders with additional coal rails to increase the capacity and the tenders paired with the earlier engines were quickly brought into line.   WWW.RAIL-ONLINE.CO.UK

Despite the addition of coal rails, a notional 5½ tons of coal and 3,500 gallons of water were still really insufficient for at least some of the duties of a 'Royal Scot' and tenders were still regularly piled high to awkward and even dangerous levels. It was therefore decided in late 1935 that the Class should have the larger Stanier 4,000 gallon, 9 ton type. Initially, tenders were exchanged with 'Jubilees', but over thirty engines had newly built tenders. Before being paired with the 'Scot' the height of the front platform was altered and the brake cylinder reduced in diameter with a liner to maintain designed brake force at 250 psi. This picture of 46139 The Welch Regiment at Canton shed, Cardiff after working a Welch Regiment special from Portsmouth on 31st October 1960 illustrates the 4,000 gallon riveted type most commonly used with the 'Scots', although a few engines had tenders with welded tanks.   R.O. TUCK/RAIL ARCHIVE STEPHENSON

PICTORIAL SUPPLEMENT

No. 46112 Sherwood Forester at Nottingham shed on 18th September 1948, following a heavy general repair, illustrates the LNWR-style lined black that was used for full repaints between April 1948 and the autumn of 1949. Even the fine red lining is apparent, which is often not the case in monochrome pictures. Points of interest include the early type of plain axlebox covers on the tender, the fact that all of the engine's wheels were original pattern, and the experiment plaque on the cab footstep support, for which we have no positive explanation. The tender lettering was the larger of the sizes used at that time and was hand painted.
T.G. HEPBURN/RAIL ARCHIVE STEPHENSON

The final condition of the class is shown by 46162 Queen's Westminster Rifleman at Patricroft in late 1962 or early 1963. It had AWS and a Smith-Stone speed indicator and was in the final lined green livery which all of the class eventually received; overhead live wire warning plates had been fixed on the deflectors, boiler and firebox. The tender with its post-1956 crest is unusual because it was one of the smaller 3,500 gallon Stanier type which carried only 7 tons of coal. This tender was paired with 46104 in 1937 and was transferred to 46162 in March 1961, remaining with it until withdrawal in May 1964.   WWW.RAIL-ONLINE.CO.UK

PRE-WAR

The first fifty 'Scots' were immediately put to use on the principal Western and Northern Division expresses. In addition to The Royal Scot and other Anglo-Scottish services, the most important trains on the Liverpool, Manchester and Holyhead routes became principally 'Scot' hauled. The additional twenty Derby-built engines in 1930 further reduced double-heading and banking, as well as providing appropriate motive power for increased summer traffic.

In the early 1930s, LMS express services were accelerated, notably the Anglo-Scottish trains following the termination of a long-standing agreement with the LNER in 1932. Other notable accelerations were on the Liverpool and Manchester trains with the fastest scheduled at over a mile-per-minute, with the 5/25pm from Liverpool becoming the fastest rail journey in Europe in excess of 150 miles, covering the 152½ miles from Crewe to Willesden at an average of 64.4 mph. The Mancunian was the longest run in Europe at over a mile a minute, covering the 177 miles from Wilmslow to Euston at 61.7 mph. Both trains were hauled by 'Royal Scots'.

Despite the steadily increasing train weights and speeds the 'Scots' continued to perform well, but the demands made of them began to expose their weaknesses as well and problems such as hot axleboxes, frame cracks and leaking smokeboxes mentioned earlier became significant. However, until sufficient Pacifics became available in the late 1930s they continued to bear the brunt of the principal LMS long-distance expresses.

During a visit to America in April 1930, the LMS President Sir Josiah Stamp met Rufus Dawes, who was president of the board in charge of promoting and organising a Century of Progress exposition in Chicago due to open on 1st June 1933. As a result, the LMS was invited in 1932 to send a locomotive and train to the exposition and since none of the new 'Princess Royal' Pacifics would be ready in time, a 'Royal Scot' was sent. This purported to be the original 6100 Royal Scot but we believe it swapped identities permanently while in Crewe Works with the newer Derby-built 6152 before leaving for the USA.

From 1935 Stanier's Pacifics replaced the 'Scots' on prestige workings such as The Royal Scot, Midday Scot and Night Scot, as well as some of the Liverpool expresses. However, they still hauled other expresses, newspaper specials, fish trains, milk trains, express or fitted freights that needed powerful engines able to maintain tight timings.

Most of the Class were fitted with speed recorders from 1936, and more than twenty ran briefly in the 1936 sans serif livery. As previously stated, the crosshead driven vacuum pumps and bogie brakes were taken off, and they all acquired Stanier 9 ton 4,000 gallon tenders in place of the 'Old Standard' 3,500 gallon type.

An immaculate 6139 Ajax *departing from Carlisle Citadel with the* Up Royal Scot *in 1931, the year before the train, together with other principal LMS expresses, was significantly accelerated. Its tender had not yet been fitted with additional coal rails and the coal had been piled as high as the loading gauge permitted. This was normal practice, especially before the engines were fitted with multiple valve piston rings which materially improved their fuel consumption. According to an ex-Camden driver it was not unknown for the fireman to be, 'Brushing the dust out of the back', at the end of the 300 miles journey. No. 6139 was renamed* The Welch Regiment *in March 1936.*

F.R. HEBRON/RAIL ARCHIVE STEPHENSON

PICTORIAL SUPPLEMENT

No. 6158 The Loyal Regiment *on Bushey troughs when working the Up* Ulster Express *in August 1931. It was picking up water even though this was the nearest set of troughs to Euston.*
GEORGE R. GRIGS/RAIL ARCHIVE STEPHENSON

No. 6160 passing over Castlethorpe water troughs with the Up Royal Scot *in late 1932 after it was transferred from Holyhead to Carlisle Upperby. It had the early flat pattern of smoke deflectors and its tender was built with additional coal rails. Seven of the engines built at Derby in 1930, including 6160, were still to receive their names at the end of 1932. The white-painted hinges and rim on the smokebox door and the polished buffers contrast with the paintwork of the tender.*
H. GORDON TIDEY/RAIL ARCHIVE STEPHENSON COLLECTION

THE 'ROYAL SCOTS'

No. 6104 Scottish Borderer on arrival at Euston in around 1935. It had angled smoke deflectors with the commode handles moved onto the lower part of the deflector plates ahead of the drop portion of the front platform. The tender had additional coal rails which were fitted in May 1932, and the bogie brakes had been removed. No. 6104 was from Polmadie where it had been allocated since March 1931. RAIL ARCHIVE STEPHENSON

In mid-1938 the 'Scots' started to work the 5.50 pm London-Birmingham express, having been rarely seen on the West Midlands trains up to that time. No. 6114 Coldstream Guardsman was photographed passing its home shed at Camden with a Euston to Wolverhampton express in 1938. It was in 1936 livery applied during a Heavy General overhaul completed in March 1937 and had a Stanier tender dating from August 1936 and a side bolster bogie fitted in 1935. Coldstream Guardsman was the engine involved in the Leighton Buzzard accident in March 1931 which was a major factor leading to the fitting of smoke deflectors to the whole class within a year.
C.R.L. COLES/RAIL ARCHIVE STEPHENSON

The London to Manchester expresses including the Comet and Mancunian were worked by the 'Scots' throughout the 1930s and were timed at start-to-stop average speeds of over 60 m.p.h. Although Longsight received five of the Derby-built engines the London work was shared with Camden whose 6109 Royal Engineer was photographed approaching Tring with a Euston to Manchester London Road express in 1938. Underneath the grime the 1936 sans serif stock numbers applied in early 1937 can just be discerned, as can the plain, rectangular cross-section coupling rods. The angled smoke deflectors had a round rather than the usual flat beading and the commode handle was on the lower part of the plates.
C.R.L. COLES/RAIL ARCHIVE STEPHENSON

No. 6142 The York and Lancashire Regiment *with the Up Manxman from Liverpool to London near Whitmore in around 1938. It was allocated to Edge Hill shed from November 1927 until 1939 and had the final pattern of round top smoke deflectors with the main portions of the deflector plates moved further out from the smokebox, still with a gentle curve to the top, with the lower part in front of the platform drop section. The stock numbers on the cab were the large 14in type, replacing the short-lived 1936 sans serif numbers on 6142.* RAIL ARCHIVE STEPHENSON

No. 6146 The Rifle Brigade *had the same deflectors and livery as 6142 when also photographed near Whitmore with a Barrow-in-Furness to Euston express in c.1938. The thirteen-coach load was typical for 'Scots' on pre-war West Coast Main Line services. No. 6146 was stationed at Crewe North from October 1935 until April 1940.* RAIL ARCHIVE STEPHENSON

No. 6118 Royal Welch Fusilier *at Crewe with the Up* Irish Mail *in the late-1930s after it was paired with a Stanier tender in April 1936. From around 1932 Holyhead had around half a dozen 'Scots' on its books for working the expresses between Holyhead and Euston including 6118 which was transferred between there and Crewe North four times during the 1930s.* T.G. HEPBURN/RAIL ARCHIVE STEPHENSON

No. 6138 The London Irish Rifleman *with an Up milk train at Crewe in around 1938. It had been transferred to Carlisle Upperby in September 1937. By this date, the Class had been supplanted on much of its prestige work by Stanier Pacifics and although they still hauled many expresses, they were also used on newspaper specials, fish trains, milk trains, express or fitted freights that needed powerful engines able to maintain tight timings.* T.G. HEPBURN/RAIL ARCHIVE STEPHENSON

THE 'ROYAL SCOTS'

Crewe North's 6113 Cameronian climbing Shap unassisted with a twelve coach Down express on 27th August 1937. It exhibits some of the modifications applied to the class in the 1930s with a Stanier 4,000 gallon tender and angled smoke deflectors but it still had a crosshead vacuum pump and additional rainstrips had not yet been fitted on the cab roof. On 27th April 1928 6113 ran non-stop with The Royal Scot from Euston to Glasgow as the LMS successfully took the wind out of the LNER's publicity sails by pre-empting the latter's much heralded non-stop Kings Cross – Edinburgh Flying Scotsman service which was due to start the following month.
COLLING TURNER/RAIL ARCHIVE STEPHENSON

Another Crewe North engine, 6153 The Royal Dragoon, *had an easier climb with only eight coaches as it ascended Shap with a Down express in 1937.*
COLLING TURNER/RAIL ARCHIVE STEPHENSON

Camden's 6114 Coldstream Guardsman *climbing Shap at Greenholme with a Down express in 1938. Changes apparent since the previous picture of the engine at Camden include the final curved top pattern of smoke deflectors and the removal of the crosshead vacuum pump, both modifications carried out during a works visit in April/May 1938.*
COLLING TURNER/RAIL ARCHIVE STEPHENSON

No. 6160 Queen Victoria's Rifleman at Prestatyn with a Holyhead express on 25th July 1939. It was one of five new Derby built engines allocated to Holyhead in 1930 for working the expresses to London. After two years 6160 moved away for brief spells at Carlisle and Camden before going to Crewe North in late 1933 where it remained until returning to Holyhead in 1940. T.G. HEPBURN/RAIL ARCHIVE STEPHENSON

Bangor was home to eleven different 'Scots' during the 1930s, one of which was 6113 Cameronian photographed waiting to depart from Holyhead in August 1938. It had just been transferred there from Crewe North in July, which is probably why it had a temporary square shed plate inscribed with the number 7. It still had angled smoke deflectors but the crosshead vacuum pump had been removed and there were additional rainstrips on the cab roof. WWW.RAIL-ONLINE.CO.UK

1940s

After War broke out in September 1939 the 'Scots' worked many different types of traffic. In many instances loads exceeded those seen up to 1939 and seventeen coaches on London to Liverpool and Manchester trains became quite common. The most important development during the war, though, was of course the start of the rebuilding programme in 1943. One of the main reasons for the 'Scots' being converted was so that they could work on the Midland Division. The first of these went to Leeds to work over the Leeds to Carlisle line and by the end of 1944 five were stationed at Holbeck. However, the original intention to allocate the rebuilds to the Midland Division then changed, and most ended up on the Western Division and at nationalisation there were still only the five at Holbeck.

Shortly after Britain's railways were nationalised on 1st January 1948, a series of dynamometer car trials was carried out to compare the best locomotives from each of the former companies. In the express passenger category there were five types – LMS 'Coronation', LNER A4 and Southern Railway 'Merchant Navy' Pacifics, and GWR 'King' and the LMS 'Royal Scot' 4-6-0s. The routes chosen for testing were Waterloo to Exeter, King's Cross to Leeds, Euston to Carlisle and Paddington to Plymouth, with 500 ton trains on the first two and 450 tons on the LMS and GWR lines. The 'Royal Scots' were the smallest and notionally least powerful engines in the category. Many people were surprised at their inclusion but they outperformed the 'Kings', came close to some of the running of the Pacifics and laid the foundation for the claim that they were the best 4-6-0s ever to run on British metals.

Some of the 'Scots' were repainted in wartime plain black livery including the first conversions but ten parallel boiler engines managed to retain their crimson lake until well after the end of the War, some even into nationalisation. The engines repainted after the War carried two of the three new liveries that were introduced during this period – firstly LMS 1946 lined black and then from April 1948, BR lined black. Uniformity was restored from August 1949 onwards when all repainted engines received the new BR standard green express passenger livery.

No. 6136 The Border Regiment *with an Up express passing the distinctive masts of the Rugby Radio Station at Hillmorton near Rugby. It had the third pattern of smoke deflectors, having had the early flat type, then the later angled pattern before ending with the curved top ones shown in this picture. It had been transferred to Edge Hill in 1943 from Camden.*

WWW.RAIL-ONLINE.CO.UK

No. 6116 Irish Guardsman *had plenty of steam to spare as it prepared to depart from Crewe in early 1948. It was rebuilt with a taper boiler in May 1944 and had been allocated to Camden since mid-1940; its BR number was not applied until September 1948.* WWW.RAIL-ONLINE.CO.UK

M6138 The London Irish Rifleman *at Glasgow Central in 1948 was one of only a few 1946 style lined black locomotives which had the short-lived M prefix applied to their LMS numbers introduced at nationalisation to indicate that they were previously owned by the LMS or, in the case of new locomotives, that they had been designed by the LMS. This only lasted until March 1948 when the system was changed and London Midland Region engines had 40,000 added to their numbers instead. A plate with the M prefix had been added on a small extension piece riveted in front of the number, the letter being also scroll and serif to match the numbers; 6138 was the only 'Scot' to have this. On the cab side the prefix was actually displayed as a 6in high suffix below the stock number.* WWW.RAIL-ONLINE.CO.UK

Two 'Scots' represented the London Midland Region in the Express Passenger category of the Locomotive Interchange Trials carried out by newly formed British Railways in 1948. One of these was 46162 Queen's Westminster Rifleman, photographed when passing West Drayton & Yiewsley with the 1.30pm Paddington to Plymouth express in May 1948. No. 46162 was also used in the tests on the LMR between Euston and Carlisle and on the Eastern Region between Kings Cross and Leeds, alongside A4, 'Coronation' and 'Merchant Navy' Pacifics and the GWR 'King' 4-6-0. The engines selected were to have run between 15,000 and 20,000 miles since the last general repair and each was to be specially examined before leaving the parent Region to minimise repairs during the trials. A well-groomed 46162 had a scroll and serif smokebox door numberplate and 10in 1946-style cabside numerals with 14in unshaded sans serif LMS on the tender.
C.R.L. COLES/RAIL ARCHIVE STEPHENSON

Although it was intended that the same engine of each class should work throughout the trials, 46154 The Hussar was used instead of 46162 on the Southern Region tests between Waterloo and Exeter. It was photographed arriving at Waterloo with the 'Atlantic Coast Express' on 16th June 1948, paired with a WD 'Austerity' 5,000 gallon tender because there were no water troughs available on that route. The 'Royal Scots' were the smallest and notionally least powerful engines in the Express Passenger category. Many people were surprised at their inclusion in the trials but they outperformed the 'Kings', came close to some of the running of the Pacifics and laid the foundation for the claim that they were the best 4-6-0s ever to run on British metals.
C.R.L. COLES/RAIL ARCHIVE STEPHENSON

THE 'ROYAL SCOTS'

In early British Railways days, the class were not frequent visitors to Birmingham although Crewe North's 6113 Cameronian was photographed at New Street on 24th January 1949. It was still in LMS 1946 livery and was not renumbered until the following May; it was converted at the end of 1950. WWW.RAIL-ONLINE.CO.UK

No. 46106 Gordon Highlander running over Newbold troughs as it headed south on the West Coast Main Line towards Rugby, probably in the early part of 1949; the engine was rebuilt between June and September of that year. It had been renumbered in June 1948 whilst still in crimson lake livery and initially had LMS-style block cab numbers but by this date these had been changed to 8in Gill Sans numbers. The smokebox number was in block style and the tender still had LMS lettering. No. 46106 remained in this condition until rebuilt when it emerged in BR green. WWW.RAIL-ONLINE.CO.UK

46141 The North Staffordshire Regiment restarting from a signal check at Kilsby & Crick in 1949 with a Sunday express for Euston diverted via Northampton. Underneath the grime, it was in BR lined black with BRITISH RAILWAYS tender lettering and large block style cab numbers dating from July 1948. It had been allocated to Camden since November 1947 and was converted to a taper boiler in October 1950.
W.J. VERDEN ANDERSON/RAIL ARCHIVE STEPHENSON

THE 'ROYAL SCOTS'

Edge Hill's 46164 *The Artists' Rifleman* with an Up express alongside the Oxford Canal at Brinklow in 1949. It had been renumbered in April 1948 while still in crimson lake livery, but it had been repainted in BR lined black with BRITISH RAILWAYS tender lettering during a Heavy General repair completed in September 1948; 46164 was converted to a taper boiler in June 1951. WWW.RAIL-ONLINE.CO.UK

Longsight's 46149 The Middlesex Regiment *on a northbound express at Brinklow shortly before it was fitted with smoke deflectors in November 1949. Underneath the grime it was in BR lined black with 8in Gill Sans stock numbers and 8¾ in BRITISH RAILWAYS tender letters. No. 46149 had been converted in April 1945 and received its BR number in April 1948 with a scroll and serif smokebox number plate.*

WWW.RAIL-ONLINE.CO.UK

No. 46141 The North Staffordshire Regiment *at Hillmorton near Rugby in 1949. It had been renumbered in June 1948 with a Gill Sans smokebox door plate, 10in 1946 block style stock numbers and 8¾ in BRITISH RAILWAYS on the tender. Livery was 1946 lined black which it retained until converted in October 1950 and the engine was allocated to Camden from November 1947 until 1951.*

WWW.RAIL-ONLINE.CO.UK

THE 'ROYAL SCOTS'

One of the early conversions in June 1944, 46138 The London Irish Rifleman approaching Rugby with an Up express after it was renumbered in January 1949. It was in LMS 1946 livery with its BR stock number in 8in Gill Sans numerals and similar smokebox plate with 10in BRITISH RAILWAYS on the tender. The engine was allocated to Edge Hill from August 1940 until September 1951 when it moved to Holyhead.
W.J. VERDEN ANDERSON/RAIL ARCHIVE STEPHENSON

PICTORIAL SUPPLEMENT

As part of British Railways' deliberations on liveries for its locomotives and rolling stock, 46139 The Welch Regiment had its BR number applied and was painted during conversion to taper boiler in May 1948 in a shade described at the time as LNER Apple Green. The lining was similar to the BR lined black with the difference that between the cream and red lining was green and only the leading splashers were lined. In the event, that colour was not chosen and no other 'Scot' was so treated; 46139 probably remained in this livery until its next heavy general repair which commenced in April 1950. The smokebox door numberplate and the 8in cabside numerals with power class below were Gill Sans, as was the 10in BRITISH RAILWAYS on the tender sides. No. 46139 was fitted with smoke deflectors in September 1950.
WWW.RAIL-ONLINE.CO.UK

46143 The South Staffordshire Regiment was taking water from Rugby troughs with a Down express in 1949, the year in which it was converted. Hence it was in BR lined black which was used on the conversions completed between April 1948 and about October 1949. Numbers and lettering were Gill Sans, 8in on the cab and 10in BRITISH RAILWAYS on the tender. No. 46143 was at Polmadie until rebuilt, moving to Longsight when it left Crewe Works in June 1949.

W.J. VERDEN ANDERSON/RAIL ARCHIVE STEPHENSON

No. 46158 The Loyal Regiment from Crewe North with an Up express at Hillmorton south of Rugby, probably in 1949. It was in LMS 1946 livery, modified in October 1948 with British Railways stock numbers in 10in block numerals and a Gill Sans smokebox plate; it was converted in late 1952.

W.J. VERDEN ANDERSON/RAIL ARCHIVE STEPHENSON

The first of the converted engines went to Leeds to work over the Midland Division route to Carlisle and by the end of 1944 five of them, 6103, 6108, 6109, 6117 and 6133, were allocated to Holbeck. The original idea of having the bulk of the converted engines allocated to the Midland Division then changed and the majority ended up on the Western Division. At nationalisation on 1st January 1948 there remained only five of the taper boiler examples on the Midland Division, all at Holbeck where they did some of the finest work ever seen in steam days over the Leeds – Settle – Carlisle line with such trains as the Thames – Clyde Express. Holbeck still had five of the class in 1960, including 46117 Welsh Guardsman, converted at the end of 1943, and pictured at Hellifield with a northbound express in around 1949. It had been renumbered in May 1948 with a scroll and serif smokebox plate and 10in block style cab numbers. J.W. HAGUE/RAIL ARCHIVE STEPHENSON

THE 'ROYAL SCOTS'

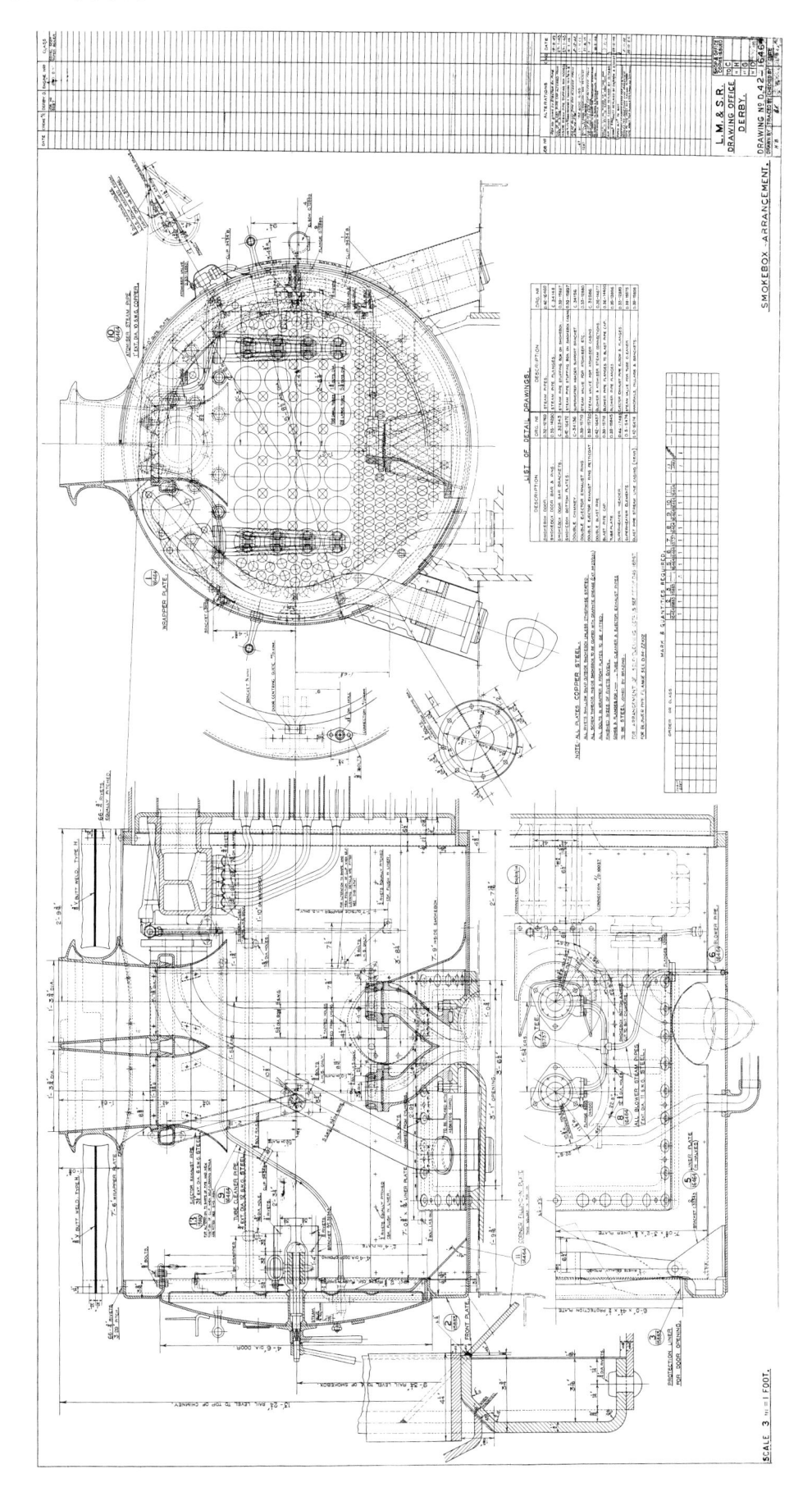

D42-16464 – Smokebox Arrangement – converted engines

This drawing, which was supplied by our LMS Society colleague Bob Meanley, was omitted from the Profile because of space considerations. It shows the arrangement of the smokebox on a 'standard' converted engine without self-cleaning apparatus or the draughting alterations carried out on a few locomotives following the Rugby Test Plant results of 1955.

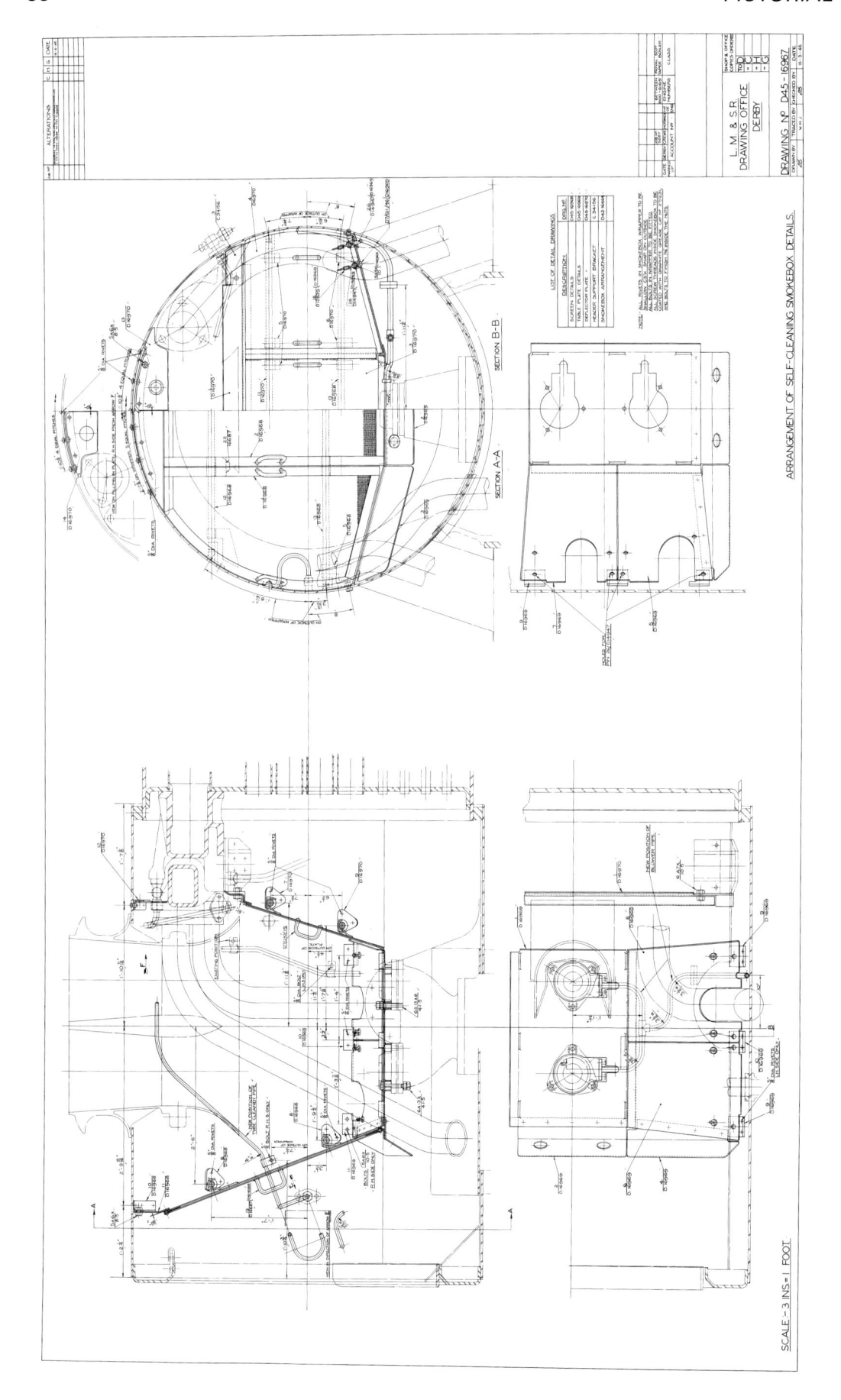

D45-16967 - Arrangement of Self-Cleaning Smokebox Details - converted engines

Also provided by Bob Meanley and omitted from the Profile, this drawing shows the arrangement tried during the 1940s when self-cleaning apparatus was fitted to some engines without any modification to the draughting. This proved detrimental to steaming and following the 1955 Rugby tests a different arrangement of the apparatus together with some alteration of the draughting was fitted to a few engines. A sketch of that arrangement, together with those showing the two arrangements seen here, can be seen on page 77 of the Profile together with a more detailed account of the tests and trial fittings on page 79 et seq of that work.

THE 'ROYAL SCOTS'

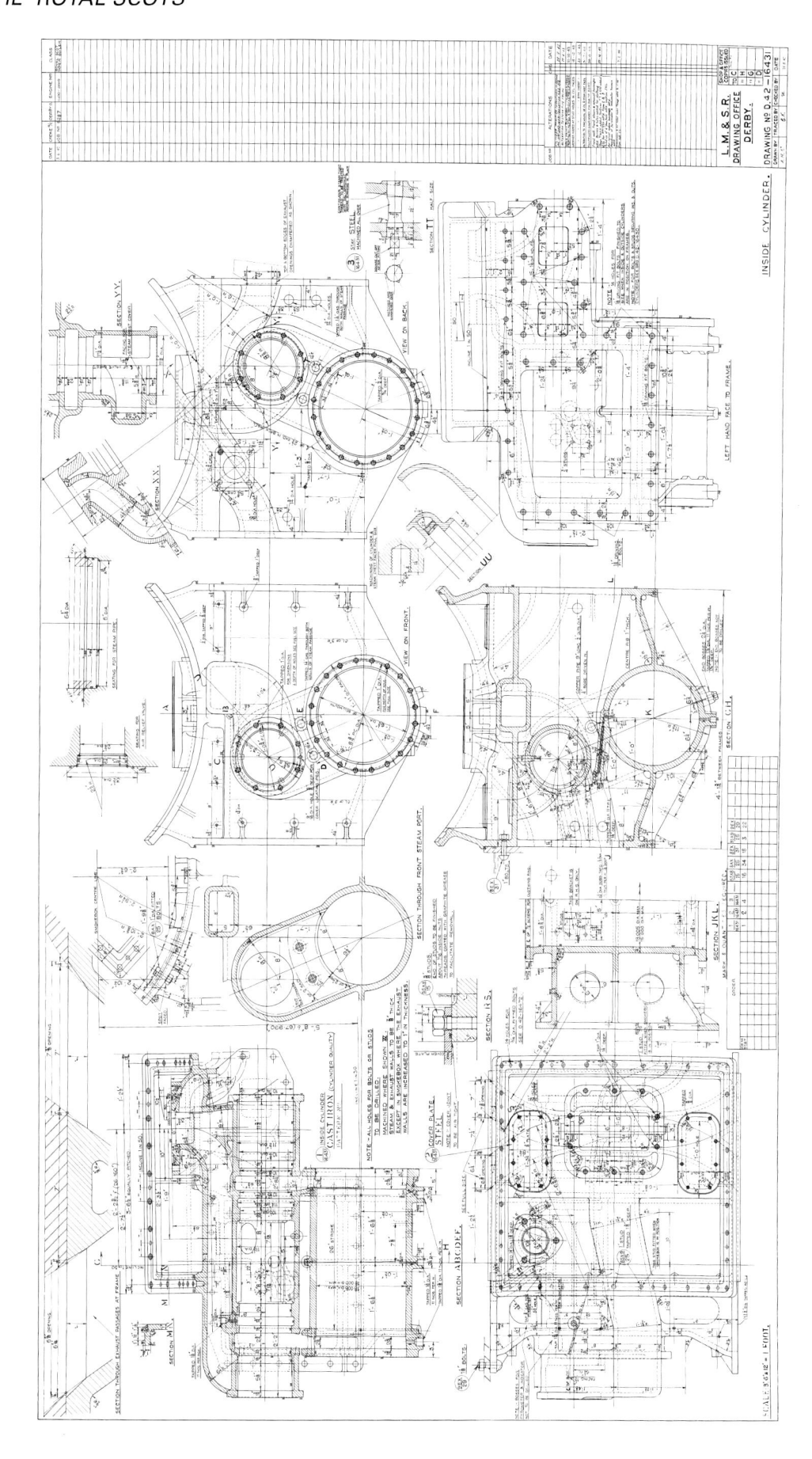

D42-16431 – Inside Cylinder Arrangement – converted engines

The third of the drawings provided by Bob Meanley that we did not include in the Profile is this one showing the inside cylinder arrangement of the converted, or rebuilt, locomotives. The adoption of the new boiler and the use of a cylindrical smokebox meant that new inside cylinder castings incorporating the smokebox saddle had to be designed. The opportunity was then taken to improve the cylinder and valve arrangement and the Chief Draughtsman, Tom Coleman, had designs drawn up for new inside and outside 18in cylinders with 9in piston valves, streamlined passages and larger ports. Such features are shown here.

EARLY 1950s

At nationalisation fourteen of the Class remained to be converted and it was not until 1955 that the final example received its taper boiler. Six of the unrebuilt engines went to Bushbury in late 1950 to work the Wolverhampton-Euston trains but all left in July 1951. Apart from this there were only minor changes in the allocations, confined almost entirely to movements between the principal Western Division sheds. From January 1949 Edge Hill 'Scots' began to appear regularly on the Trans-Pennine services to Leeds, Hull and Newcastle in place of 'Jubilees' and unrebuilt 'Patriots' and they continued in their role supporting the Pacifics, primarily on the Western Division, for the first half of the decade.

West Coast main line

With the British Thomson-Houston works in the background, 46138 The London Irish Rifleman was photographed approaching Rugby station with an Up express for Euston in March 1950, six months before it was fitted with smoke deflectors. It had Stanier pattern plain section fish-bellied coupling rods. British Thomson-Houston had produced heavy electrical equipment such as electric motors and generators on the site since 1902, the Company having been founded in 1894 and production started at Rugby in 1900. BTH amalgamated with Metropolitan Vickers to form Associated Electrical Industries (AEI) in 1928, although the name British Thomson-Houston continued to be used until 1960.
W.J. VERDEN ANDERSON/RAIL ARCHIVE STEPHENSON

THE 'ROYAL SCOTS'

The last engine built, 46169 The Boy Scout, was converted in May 1945 and the smoke deflectors were fitted in January 1950. It was allocated to Longsight from October 1946 until July 1959, which suggests that in this picture at Brinklow it was probably working a Manchester to London express.
WWW.RAIL-ONLINE.CO.UK

No. 46110 Grenadier Guardsman on a Down express running parallel with the Oxford Canal at Brinklow was still in LMS 1946 livery with LMS lettering on the tender. It had been renumbered in May 1948 with a Gill Sans smokebox plate and 8in Gill Sans cab numbers. This picture was taken while it was allocated to Carlisle Upperby, between July 1951 and April 1952, after which it was transferred to Crewe North. WWW.RAIL-ONLINE.CO.UK

THE 'ROYAL SCOTS'

Rebuilt 46114 Coldstream Guardsman on an Up express at Hillmorton south of Rugby. It had been converted in 1946 but was not fitted with smoke deflectors until September 1950. It became No. 46114 in June 1948, with block pattern numerals on the smokebox numberplate but with 8in Gill Sans cab numbers. It was allocated to Manchester Longsight until May 1955 when it was transferred to Camden. The first vehicle was an LMS Period One all-third coach fitted with Stones ventilators; it had been added as a 'strengthener' to provide additional seating. WWW.RAIL-ONLINE.CO.UK

PICTORIAL SUPPLEMENT

The last of the class to be rebuilt with a taper boiler, 46137 The Prince of Wales's Volunteers (South Lancashire) passing the Hillmorton masts near Rugby in 1950 with a southbound express when still in plain black with no lettering on the tender. It was originally named Vesta, was renamed in May 1936 and received its British Railways number in May 1948 with a scroll & serif type smokebox numberplate and 10in LMS 1946 style cabside numbers. Just as with No.46114 overleaf, an elderly Period One all third 'strengthener' had been added at the front of the train.
WWW.RAIL-ONLINE.CO.UK

THE 'ROYAL SCOTS'

No. 46115 Scots Guardsman comes round the curve to the north of Rugby with a Down West Coast Main Line express in March 1950 in LMS 1946 livery and still carrying LMS tender lettering. Its BR number was not applied until January 1949 using 8in Gill Sans stock numbers and smokebox plate. The engine had been converted in August 1947 and was fitted as a trial with a new type of smoke deflector that had raked back leading edges, were shorter than those used previously on the parallel boiler engines, mounted closer to the smokebox and curved round it. John Powell was detailed to ride on the engine and report on the deflectors' effectiveness. He was totally unimpressed and said so in his report, but the Motive Power Department expressed complete satisfaction with them and commencing in September 1949 they were fitted to all the other converted 'Scots'.
W.J. VERDEN ANDERSON/RAIL ARCHIVE STEPHENSON

No. 46115 Scots Guardsman was taking water from Castlethorpe troughs, north of Wolverton, when photographed with a Down express from Euston on 7th May 1955. It was at Longsight from late 1949 until 1960 and was purchased for preservation by Mr. R. A. Bill following withdrawal on 1st January 1966. After being kept for a time on the Keighley & Worth Valley Railway it moved to the Dinting Railway Centre in 1969 where it was repaired and returned briefly to main line operation during 1979 painted in 1946 LMS lined black. A change in the boiler regulations by British Rail meant that after only a few outings the engine was confined to Dinting. On the demise of the Dinting Railway Centre it led a somewhat nomadic existence as a kit of parts before being taken in by the North of England Railway Historical Trust. It then underwent a general repair to main line standard that was completed at Carnforth and was painted BR green by July 2008. Scots Guardsman then ran regularly on the main line until its boiler certificate expired in 2017. D.M.C. HEPBURNE-SCOTT/RAIL ARCHIVE STEPHENSON

THE 'ROYAL SCOTS'

The Permanent Way men can be seen exchanging greetings with the fireman of an immaculate 46127 Old Contemptibles near Basford Sidings as it started the climb up to Whitmore troughs with a Glasgow-Birmingham express. The 156 milepost shows that this was just two miles south of Crewe station. No. 46127 was converted in 1944 and was fitted with smoke deflectors in August 1951. It still carried an 8A Edge Hill shedplate although records show it left there in 1947.
RAIL ARCHIVE STEPHENSON

48 PICTORIAL SUPPLEMENT

No. 46143 The South Staffordshire Regiment was watched by a crowd of 'spotters as it prepared to leave Crewe with a Down express. It received BR lined black livery after conversion in June 1949. This picture was taken while it was allocated to Camden, between March 1951 and September 1952.
KENNETH FIELD/RAIL ARCHIVE STEPHENSON

THE 'ROYAL SCOTS'

No. 46167 The Hertfordshire Regiment was about to add a Palethorpes van to its train at the north end of Crewe station in late 1951 or early 1952. Converted at the end of 1948, it had been transferred to Crewe North from Longsight in December 1951 and ran without smoke deflectors until August 1952. It was in the LNWR-style lined black used on the engines converted between about April 1948 and October 1949 and had a Gill Sans smokebox plate, 8in cab numbers and tender lettering. The 6P power classification of the 'Scots' was changed to 7P in 1951, the 2in figures being positioned above rather than below the stock numbers as on 46116.

WWW.RAIL-ONLINE.CO.UK

In pre-war days the Edge Hill 'Scots' worked many of the Liverpool–London trains and from January 1949 they also began to appear regularly on the Trans-Pennine services to Leeds, Hull and Newcastle. No. 46132 The King's Regiment Liverpool was waiting to depart from Liverpool Lime Street in the mid-1950s as the fireman did some last minute work on the tender top. The Edge Hill engine had been converted with a taper boiler in late 1943 and was fitted with smoke deflectors in October 1951. Except for a couple of months at Longsight it was at the Liverpool shed from October 1954 until September 1959, when it moved to the Midland Division at Kentish Town.
KENNETH FIELD/RAIL ARCHIVE STEPHENSON

THE 'ROYAL SCOTS'

The penultimate taper boiler conversion, 46148 The Manchester Regiment, *arriving at Manchester London Road on 24th January 1954, less than a month before it went into Crewe Works for conversion. It was one of only a handful of parallel boiler engines to be repainted in BR lined green, a livery which it had from November 1950.*

WWW.RAIL-ONLINE.CO.UK

No. 46135 The East Lancashire Regiment *is here heading a very motley collection of passenger stock which was so typical of the early British Railways period. It was on the Up Main at Boars Head, north of Wigan in the early-1950s, and was allocated to Edge Hill from before it was converted in January 1947 up to April 1954.*

WWW.RAIL-ONLINE.CO.UK

52 PICTORIAL SUPPLEMENT

In this picture 46125 3rd Carabinier was climbing away from Oxenholme with a Down express at the start of the long haul up to Shap with the Windermere branch curving away on the right. It was one of the early taper boiler conversions, completed in August 1943 and was the most nomadic 'Scot', with no fewer than thirty-six recorded allocation changes.
J.D. MILLS/RAIL ARCHIVE STEPHENSON

THE 'ROYAL SCOTS' 53

No. 46143 The South Staffordshire Regiment was passing Scout Green signal box as it climbed Shap with a Down express in July 1956. It was in its third spell at Longsight since conversion in mid-1949.   W.J. VERDEN ANDERSON/RAIL ARCHIVE STEPHENSON

PICTORIAL SUPPLEMENT

The driver was admiring the view as 46128 The Lovat Scouts from Crewe North took the eleven coaches of a London to Glasgow express up to Shap summit without the need for banking assistance. It had just passed the Intermediate Block signal (visible after the last coach) at Shap Wells that was controlled by the tiny signal box at Scout Green crossing, 1 1/3 miles back down the incline. WWW.RAIL-ONLINE.CO.UK

THE 'ROYAL SCOTS'

Chester and North Wales

On the first taper boiler conversions the original sanding gear was not modified, with sand pipes only in front of the leading coupled wheels and either side of the middle ones. However, following some instances of bent coupling rods when sanding was applied during a slip, it was decided in March 1945 that extra pipes be installed ahead of the trailing wheels and large double sand boxes were fitted on top of the platform adjacent to the firebox. These are prominent in this picture of 46132 The King's Regiment Liverpool *as it waited to leave Chester with a Down express.*
KENNETH FIELD/RAIL ARCHIVE STEPHENSON

No. 46127 Old Contemptibles *approaching Penryhn Siding east of Bethesda Junction, Bangor with a Down slow in 1951. It had been transferred to Holyhead in March of that year and still had a 7C shedplate which was changed to 6J in March 1952.*
J.D. MILLS/RAIL ARCHIVE STEPHENSON

PICTORIAL SUPPLEMENT

North East

The rebuilt 'Scots' allocated to Holbeck during the 1950s mostly worked to the north of Leeds over the Settle – Carlisle line with such trains as The Thames – Clyde Express. No. 46108 Seaforth Highlander passing Whitehall Junction as it left Leeds with the Down service. It was fitted with smoke deflectors and painted in BR lined green during a Heavy General repair completed in February 1951 and was at Holbeck only until December 1952.
KENNETH FIELD/RAIL ARCHIVE STEPHENSON

THE 'ROYAL SCOTS'

This picture shows 46123 Royal Irish Fusilier *emerging from Standedge tunnel with the 9am Liverpool Lime Street to Newcastle express. It was allocated to Edge Hill from March 1948, was converted in May 1949 and had the welded tender shown in this picture from April 1953.* KENNETH FIELD/RAIL ARCHIVE STEPHENSON

Another Edge Hill rebuilt 'Scot', 46152 The King's Dragoon Guardsman *passing Springwood Junction, Huddersfield with the 9am Newcastle to Liverpool Lime Street express in October 1953.* KENNETH FIELD/RAIL ARCHIVE STEPHENSON

LATE 1950s AND EARLY 1960s

As dieselisation gathered pace in the late 1950s the 'Scots', like most other express passenger steam locomotives, began to be displaced from their previous front-line duties. In late 1957, they finally appeared regularly at the southern end of the Midland Division when six were transferred to Kentish Town in October, followed by two more a year later and another ten in 1959 as the Western Division received large numbers of English Electric Type 4 diesels. However, all had gone by the autumn of 1961 as 'Peak' Type 4s took over the Midland Division express work. 'Scots' were allocated to other sheds not previously featured, for example Preston, Heaton Mersey, Willesden, Saltley, Bidston, Trafford Park, Newton Heath, Springs Branch, Derby, Nottingham, Millhouses, Leicester and Annesley. Many of the engines transferred were in extremely run-down condition, the Western Division having had the best from them.

Two final modifications were applied to most of the Class in the late-1950s and early-1960s: from January 1959 the Western Division engines were fitted with AWS and from April 1960 with Smith-Stone speed indicators; the work took place over several years.

Withdrawal started in October 1962 with 46100 *Royal Scot* itself and twenty-nine had gone by the end of that year.

West Coast main line

No. 46128 The Lovat Scouts *had steam to spare on arrival at Euston with the* Lakes Express *on 1st September 1962. It had been fitted with AWS in May 1960 and had been at Crewe North since May 1957 but would leave there for Wigan Springs Branch within the month.*　　BRIAN STEPHENSON

THE 'ROYAL SCOTS'

The new Stafford station was taking shape in the background as Crewe North's 46148 The Manchester Regiment *on the Up through road passed Fairburn '4MT' 2-6-4T No.42267 in the bay, probably in mid-1962. The power of the rebuilt 'Scots' was used to the full on the heavy expresses of the West Coast mainline, particularly given the relatively small number of Pacifics available.*　　WWW.RAIL-ONLINE.CO.UK

No. 46169 The Boy Scout *speeding under the newly installed overhead wires at Stafford with a northbound express. This was the last engine in the class, built at Derby in 1930, and had been transferred from Crewe North to Willesden in April 1962, which narrows down the date of this photograph to the middle of that year. The early LMS van on the left had been fitted with stepboards and was prominently labelled 'EM Walsall - Relaying Gang Tool Van'.*　　WWW.RAIL-ONLINE.CO.UK

60 PICTORIAL SUPPLEMENT

This view shows 46135 The East Lancashire Regiment departing from Crewe with a Sunday Blackpool Central to Euston express on 14th June 1959. It was transferred from Crewe North to Camden the following week, although it returned to 5A in September.

D.T. GREENWOOD/RAIL ARCHIVE STEPHENSON

THE 'ROYAL SCOTS'

On a very short meat train, 46136 The Border Regiment was photographed heading south from Crewe in 1961 or early 1962. It was allocated to Crewe North between October 1960 and August 1962; AWS was fitted in October 1959.
WWW.RAIL-ONLINE.CO.UK

On a more appropriate duty, 46165 The Ranger (12th London Regiment) was pulling out of Crewe at around the same date. In addition to the welded tender and a Smith-Stone speedometer, both dating from August 1960, it had AWS which was fitted in June 1959.
WWW.RAIL-ONLINE.CO.UK

PICTORIAL SUPPLEMENT

No. 46118 Royal Welch Fusilier on a northbound parcels train at Winwick, north of Warrington. It had a Carlisle Upperby shedplate, having been transferred there in June 1962. The speedometer was fitted in October 1960 and the AWS in November 1959.
WWW.RAIL-ONLINE.CO.UK

THE 'ROYAL SCOTS'

No. 46105 Cameron Highlander was making a noisy departure from Preston at 5.30pm with the combined Manchester/Liverpool to Glasgow express on 5th August 1959. It spent most of its working life in Scotland, from 1932 until withdrawal in December 1962, except for just over a year at Carlisle Kingmoor in the early days of World War Two.
D.T. GREENWOOD/RAIL ARCHIVE STEPHENSON

64 PICTORIAL SUPPLEMENT

No. 46110 Grenadier Guardsman with the 1L28 Euston-Carlisle on 11th August 1963. It had been transferred from Edge Hill to Springs Branch at the end of June but went to Carlisle Kingmoor a week later, where it saw out its days until February 1964. It had been fitted with AWS in July 1959 and a Smith-Stone speedometer in May 1960.
WWW.RAIL-ONLINE.CO.UK

THE 'ROYAL SCOTS'

Crewe North's 46155 The Lancer departing from Preston with the Down Lakes Express on 15th August 1963. In 1963 the train ran with thirteen through coaches as follows: three to Keswick/Workington, five to Windermere (with Restaurant Buffet), four to Whitehaven and one to Barrow. 46155 had been transferred to Crewe North eight times, the last occasion in June 1963 for just two months before moving away for the last time to Holyhead from where it was withdrawn in December 1964. WWW.RAIL-ONLINE.CO.UK

No. 46152 The King's Dragoon Guardsman from Holyhead shed was passing Oxenholme on 6th September 1963 working the 1S53 Crewe-Perth with an LNER horse box as its first vehicle. This was the original 6100 Royal Scot but we believe it swapped identities permanently with the newer Derby-built 6152 in 1933 because a locomotive was required to tour North America and 6100 was not in suitable condition. Expenditure of over £2,400 was authorised to prepare it for the tour – a very large sum considering that it only cost £7,750 to build the complete engine and tender in 1927. It had been fitted with AWS in September 1959 and the timing reservoir is visible on the footplate between the sandbox and the cab.
WWW.RAIL-ONLINE.CO.UK

THE 'ROYAL SCOTS'

Manchester

No. 46152 The King's Dragoon Guardsman *was leaving Manchester Exchange with a westbound express in 1960 shortly before it was fitted with a Smith-Stone speedometer. It had been at Crewe North since September 1958 and its AWS dated from April 1959.*

WWW.RAIL-ONLINE.CO.UK

No. 46124 London Scottish *pulling out of Manchester Exchange in either 1961 or 1962, probably on a Trans-Pennine service to Liverpool. It was at Edge Hill for almost fifteen years before moving to Carlisle Kingmoor in November 1962. It had been fitted with AWS in May 1959 and a speed indicator in June 1960.*

WWW.RAIL-ONLINE.CO.UK

68 PICTORIAL SUPPLEMENT

This view shows 46148 The Manchester Regiment departing westwards from Manchester Exchange during the time it was allocated to Llandudno Junction, from September 1962 until December 1963, after which it moved to Holyhead. Its AWS was fitted in May 1959 while it was allocated to Carlisle Upperby.
WWW.RAIL-ONLINE.CO.UK

THE 'ROYAL SCOTS'

Llandudno Junction's 46144 Honourable Artillery Company approaching Salford station from Manchester Exchange which can be seen in the background behind the clock tower of Sacred Trinity Church. It was at the North Wales shed for almost two years before moving to Crewe North in June 1963 for its last six months in service.
WWW.RAIL-ONLINE.CO.UK

PICTORIAL SUPPLEMENT

No. 46105 Cameron Highlander *passing Monton Green north sidings in June 1959 on the 4.15pm Manchester-Glasgow which ran via the Tyldesley branch at that time. It had been at Polmadie since 1943, five years before it was fitted with a taper boiler. The distinctive water tower of Patricroft shed can be seen on the right.*

WWW.RAIL-ONLINE.CO.UK

No. 46152 The King's Dragoon Guardsman *in 1960 at Sandersons Sidings, Worsley on the Manchester portion of a Glasgow/Edinburgh express.*

WWW.RAIL-ONLINE.CO.UK

THE 'ROYAL SCOTS'

No. 46156 *The South Wales Borderer* passing over Eccles water troughs and heading towards Manchester with an express from North Wales. It was allocated to either Holyhead or Llandudno Junction from November 1959 until October 1963, except for a few weeks at Longsight in early 1960 and at Camden in early 1963.

WWW.RAIL-ONLINE.CO.UK

In a picture probably taken after it was transferred from Crewe North to Holyhead in September 1962, 46125 *3rd Carabinier* passing through Eccles station with an eastbound express. It was originally named *Lancashire Witch* and was converted to a taper boiler in 1943; the AWS equipment was not installed until June 1961.

WWW.RAIL-ONLINE.CO.UK

West Midlands

Crewe North's 46159 The Royal Air Force *was being recorded by the local spotters as it waited to leave Birmingham New Street in 1958. It was at 5A for most of the decade, punctuated by three short spells at Camden.*
WWW.RAIL-ONLINE.CO.UK

The unmistakeable outline of 46106 Gordon Highlander, *that seems to have left all the work to the bankers as it clears the summit of the Lickey Incline at Blackwell in March 1961. It was the only one of the class with BR type smoke deflectors, fitted in 1954, which were much more effective than the smaller type which all the other rebuilt 'Scots' received. It had been equipped with AWS in October 1959 and was half-way through a six-month spell at Trafford Park shed.*
WWW.RAIL-ONLINE.CO.UK

THE 'ROYAL SCOTS'

One of eleven rebuilt Class '7Ps' – nine 'Scots' and two 'Patriots' – transferred to Saltley in mid-1961, No. 46122 Royal Ulster Rifleman was photographed at Oxford with a northbound freight on 2nd June 1962. They were probably brought in to work excursion trains in place of the '9F' 2-10-0s used in the previous year, although the Railway Observer reported that they were used on freight duties from Washwood Heath, including the ignominy of Bordesley Junction trip workings. All left within a year, mostly to Carlisle Upperby, and seven of these went almost immediately into store. No. 46122 was one of them, going north before the end of June, although it moved away to Annesley within six months.
WWW.RAIL-ONLINE.CO.UK

Chester and North Wales

A very rare double-heading of two 'Scots' as 46163 Civil Service Rifleman piloted 46120 Royal Inniskilling Fusilier on the 8.10am Holyhead-Manchester at Chester in 1960. No. 46163, which was from Holyhead shed, had been fitted with AWS in October 1959. WWW.RAIL-ONLINE.CO.UK

THE 'ROYAL SCOTS' 75

Llandudno Junction's 46144, passing Chester No.4 box with a Down express, was at the North Wales shed for almost two years before moving to Crewe North in June 1963. Honourable Artillery Company *was a much more suitable name for a modern express engine than the original one of* Ostrich.
WWW.RAIL-ONLINE.CO.UK

For many years, the meat trains from Holyhead to London Broad Street enjoyed express motive power, even Pacifics in later years. No. 46148 The Manchester Regiment *from Llandudno Junction departed from Chester with one of these in late 1962 or 1963. It had been fitted with AWS in May 1959 and a Smith-Stone speed indicator in October 1960.*
WWW.RAIL-ONLINE.CO.UK

76 PICTORIAL SUPPLEMENT

The approach to Chester General from the west was through two short tunnels and 46131 The Royal Warwickshire Regiment was photographed emerging from the first of these with an Up express in 1962. It had been transferred to Llandudno Junction from Longsight in March 1962 and this would be its final posting; it was withdrawn from there before the end of the year.
WWW.RAIL-ONLINE.CO.UK

THE 'ROYAL SCOTS'

No. 46151 The Royal Horse Guardsman waiting to leave Holyhead with an express for London. It was fitted with AWS in June 1959 while still at Crewe North before its transfer the following month to Longsight where it stayed until in February 1960 it went to Millhouses shed at Sheffield.
KENNETH FIELD/RAIL ARCHIVE STEPHENSON

Scotland

Crewe North's 46156 The South Wales Borderer *was photographed climbing Beattock with a Down express around 1957.*
W.J. VERDEN ANDERSON/RAIL ARCHIVE STEPHENSON

Although carrying express passenger headlamps, 46107 Argyll and Sutherland Highlander *had only two coaches and a full brake in tow as it left Beattock with a Carlisle to Glasgow semi-fast in around 1961. It was a Polmadie engine from 1942 until withdrawn at the end of 1962.*

THE 'ROYAL SCOTS'

No. 46140 *The King's Royal Rifle Corps*, from Newton Heath, was climbing Beattock with assistance from a banker on a northbound express on 28th April 1962. It was at the ex-Lancashire & Yorkshire shed for almost two years, between September 1961 and June 1963.
D.M.C. HEPBURNE-SCOTT/RAIL ARCHIVE STEPHENSON

PICTORIAL SUPPLEMENT

No. 46121 Highland Light Infantry, City of Glasgow Regiment taking the Stirling line at Hilton Junction south of Perth with the 12.15pm Perth to Euston express. It was originally H.L.I. until January 1949 when it was renamed and shortly afterwards moved to Polmadie where it stayed until withdrawal at the end of 1962. This picture was taken in 1959 or 1960 before it received AWS equipment in January 1961.
W.J. VERDEN ANDERSON/RAIL ARCHIVE STEPHENSON

THE 'ROYAL SCOTS'

81

On one of the express freights which always had express passenger motive power, 46106 Gordon Highlander, with its BR standard smoke deflectors, was leaving Perth with the 4.45pm fish train to the south in June 1962. At this date, five full trains conveying fish to the south left Aberdeen every day and this one departed from there at 2.15pm, splitting at Carstairs into separate portions for Birmingham and Manchester/Liverpool.

W.J. VERDEN ANDERSON/RAIL ARCHIVE STEPHENSON

82 PICTORIAL SUPPLEMENT

No. 46116 Irish Guardsman on the Stirling line at Hilton Junction south of Perth with the Perth to Euston sleeping car express. This picture was taken while it was allocated to Crewe North, from September 1958, and after it was fitted with AWS in July 1959.
D.T. GREENWOOD/RAIL ARCHIVE STEPHENSON

THE 'ROYAL SCOTS'

Midland main line

One of six 'Scots' transferred to the Midland Division at Kentish Town in October 1957. 46152 The King's Dragoon Guardsman easing away from Trent with the 4.16pm express to Manchester Central on 27th April 1958. It moved to Trafford Park in July 1958 but returned to the Western Division at Camden two weeks later when 'Britannia' Pacifics replaced the 'Scots'.
T.G. HEPBURN/RAIL ARCHIVE STEPHENSON

Two of the Holbeck engines were transferred south to Kentish Town in October 1958. One of these, 46133 The Green Howards, was taking water at Nottingham Midland when working a Leeds to St. Pancras express. It moved to its final shed, Newton Heath, in September 1961 after 'Peak' diesel-electrics had taken over the Midland Division express duties.
T.G. HEPBURN/RAIL ARCHIVE STEPHENSON

THE 'ROYAL SCOTS'

A southbound express headed by 46130 The West Yorkshire Regiment was photographed waiting to depart from Sheffield Midland after its transfer to Holbeck in December 1959; the AWS had been fitted the previous May while it was on the Western Division at Edge Hill.
WWW.RAIL-ONLINE.CO.UK

86 PICTORIAL SUPPLEMENT

On the Settle & Carlisle, 46130 The West Yorkshire Regiment climbing to Ais Gill summit with an Up express. It was at Holbeck from the end of 1959 until withdrawal in December 1962, except for a period at Low Moor in 1961/2. The 'Scots' were displaced by diesels from early 1961 on the workings north of Leeds such as the Thames-Clyde Express and The Waverley.
CECIL ORD/RAIL ARCHIVE STEPHENSON

THE 'ROYAL SCOTS'

87

No. 46153 The Royal Dragoon was photographed passing the extensive limestone quarries at Peak Forest with a Manchester-London express in 1961. It had been transferred from Bushbury to Trafford Park at the start of 1961 and left there for Annesley in February 1962. The Buxton Lime Firms Company Limited was established in 1891 by thirteen local quarry owners who merged their quarries to develop their business, increasing prices which allowed them to modernise and increase production. BLF was controlled by Brunner and Mond and subsequently became part of ICI in 1926. WWW.RAIL-ONLINE.CO.UK

THE FINAL YEARS

At the end of 1963 there were only twenty-six 'Scots' left in service, and all except five were withdrawn during 1964. The last survivor, 46115 *Scots Guardsman*, lasted until New Year's Day 1966.

In March 1962 three engines were transferred to Annesley where they worked on the semi-fast service from Nottingham to Marylebone and on parcels and freight trains over the former Great Central line. Another nine followed over the next two years but by then they were generally filthy and worn out and in April 1964 those remaining were taken off scheduled passenger duties and were even used on ballast trains and 'trip' freights, although they were used on summer Saturday excursions from the Midlands to the South Coast over the summer.

By the end of that year, the final five were concentrated at Carlisle Kingmoor where most of their work was on freight, although 46115 was noted on passenger duties during the second half of 1965. On withdrawal *Scots Guardsman* was purchased for preservation, joining 46100 *Royal Scot* which had been bought by the Butlin's Holiday Camp company in 1963. Both have been restored in recent years for main line operation, 46115 having also worked briefly on the national network during 1979.

No. 46148 The Manchester Regiment, on a Manchester-Llandudno train at Frodsham on 25th April 1964, was at either Holyhead or Llandudno Junction from Autumn 1962 until it was withdrawn in November 1964. WWW.RAIL-ONLINE.CO.UK

THE 'ROYAL SCOTS'

Great Central

No. 46101, formerly Royal Scots Grey, was passing High Wycombe with the 11.15am Nottingham Victoria to Marylebone empty newspaper vans on 15th March 1963. It had moved to Annesley from Willesden two months earlier but would only remain in service until August.
H.K. HARMAN/RAIL ARCHIVE STEPHENSON

Running without its The Boy Scout *nameplates 46169 was setting off from Nottingham Victoria with a southbound express early in 1963. It had been transferred to Annesley from Willesden in the first week of the year but still had a 1A shedplate. Despite its well-groomed appearance here, 46169 must have been in poor condition because it lasted for less than five months on the Great Central before withdrawal in May.* WWW.RAIL-ONLINE.CO.UK

Shorn of its Royal Ulster Rifleman *nameplates, 46122 was south of Rugby Central on the Neasden parcels. It was at Annesley from December 1962 until withdrawal in October 1964. Its 16B shed plate dates the photograph as post September 1963 when the shed code was changed from 16D.* WWW.RAIL-ONLINE.CO.UK

THE 'ROYAL SCOTS'

Most of the 'Scots' working on the Great Central arrived there in a run-down condition and by April 1964 had lost all of their scheduled passenger duties on the line. In this view 46112 Sherwood Forester had just passed Ruddington with a very short Up goods on 7th March 1964 only two months before its withdrawal. It was one of several engines never fitted with AWS having been based on the Midland Division, which was not equipped with the system during the 1950s and early 1960s, prior to its final transfer to Annesley in February 1962.
T.G. HEPBURN/RAIL ARCHIVE STEPHENSON

92 PICTORIAL SUPPLEMENT

During its final year of service 46156, formerly The South Wales Borderer, *departing from Woodford Halse with an Up express in early 1964. It had arrived at Annesley in October 1963 from Willesden.*
WWW.RAIL-ONLINE.CO.UK

A few months after the previous picture was taken, 46156 was photographed nearing Barnstone Tunnel, between Loughborough and East Leake, with a Down holiday express on 22nd August 1964.
T.G. HEPBURN/RAIL ARCHIVE STEPHENSON

THE 'ROYAL SCOTS'

All of the 'Scots' on the Great Central had been withdrawn by early October 1964, except for 46165 The Ranger (12th London Regiment) which lasted for another month. The white painted smokebox number plate contrasted with its appalling external condition as it worked a Class H freight at New Hucknall Sidings on 29th September 1964. It was one of the few 'Scots' to run with a 4,000 gallon welded tender which it had from August 1960 onwards.
WWW.RAIL-ONLINE.CO.UK

The final year

With the yellow cab stripe applied, indicating that the engine was not permitted to work under the live overhead wires south of Crewe from 1st September 1964, No. 46140 was waiting at Penrith in 1965. It had been transferred from Longsight to Kingmoor in October 1964 and was withdrawn from there a year later.
WWW.RAIL-ONLINE.CO.UK

THE 'ROYAL SCOTS'

The last five 'Scots' in service were all at Carlisle Kingmoor. In its last month in traffic and with nameplates removed, 46152 leaving Mauchline with the 5.30pm Glasgow St. Enoch to Carlisle in April 1965. It had moved to Kingmoor from Holyhead in January 1965.
W.J. VERDEN ANDERSON/RAIL ARCHIVE STEPHENSON

No.	Built	First name	Second name	Converted to taper boiler	BR number applied w/e	Withdrawn w/e
6100	14-08-27	Royal Scot		10-06-50	19-06-48	13-10-62
6101	11-09-27	Royal Scots Grey		16-11-45	01-05-48	31-08-63
6102	11-09-27	Black Watch		13-10-49	04-09-48	29-12-62
6103	11-09-27	Royal Scots Fusilier		26-06-43	23-10-48	22-12-62
6104	11-09-27	Scottish Borderer		30-03-46	07-08-48	29-12-62
6105	11-09-27	Cameron Highlander		27-04-48	01-05-48	29-12-62
6106	11-09-27	Gordon Highlander		21-09-49	12-06-48	08-12-62
6107	11-09-27	Argyll and Sutherland Highlander		20-02-50	03-04-48	29-12-62
6108	11-09-27	Seaforth Highlander		21-08-43	08-05-48	26-01-63
6109	11-09-27	Royal Engineer		24-07-43	01-05-48	29-12-62
6110	11-09-27	Grenadier Guardsman		31-01-53	02-04-49	22-02-64
6111	09-10-27	Royal Fusilier		01-10-47	20-11-48	28-09-63
6112	09-10-27	Sherwood Forester		14-09-43	11-09-48	09-05-64
6113	09-10-27	Cameronian		15-12-50	14-05-49	22-12-62
6114	09-10-27	Coldstream Guardsman		13-07-46	26-06-48	28-09-63
6115	09-10-27	Scots Guardsman		20-08-47	22-01-49	01-01-66
6116	09-10-27	Irish Guardsman		10-05-44	25-09-48	17-08-63
6117	06-11-27	Welsh Guardsman		09-12-43	29-05-48	01-12-62
6118	06-11-27	Royal Welch Fusilier		17-12-46	12-02-49	13-06-64
6119	06-11-27	Lancashire Fusilier		02-09-44	31-07-48	16-11-63
6120	04-12-27	Royal Inniskilling Fusilier		07-11-44	12-06-48	06-07-63
6121	06-11-27	H.L.I.	Highland Light Infantry The City of Glasgow Regiment	13-08-46	09-10-48	29-12-62
6122	06-11-27	Royal Ulster Rifleman		22-09-45	17-04-48	17-10-64
6123	06-11-27	Royal Irish Fusilier		05-05-49	26-06-48	03-11-62
6124	06-11-27	London Scottish		31-12-43	10-04-48	29-12-62
6125	11-09-27	Lancashire Witch	3rd Carabinier	07-08-43	11-09-48	03-10-64
6126	11-09-27	Sanspareil	Royal Army Service Corps	30-06-45	04-12-48	05-10-63
6127	11-09-27	Novelty	Old Contemptibles 1914 Aug. 5 to Nov. 22	02-08-44	01-05-48	08-12-62
6128	11-09-27	Meteor	The Lovat Scouts	04-06-46	26-02-49	01-05-65
6129	06-11-27	Comet	The Scottish Horse	29-11-44	26-06-48	06-06-64
6130	06-11-27	Liverpool	The West Yorkshire Regiment	06-12-49	22-05-48	22-12-62
6131	11-09-27	Planet	The Royal Warwickshire Regiment	14-10-44	07-08-48	03-11-62
6132	11-09-27	Phoenix	The King's Regiment (Liverpool)	05-11-43	24-04-48	01-02-64
6133	09-10-27	Vulcan	The Green Howards	01-07-44	29-01-49	23-02-63
6134	09-10-27	Atlas	The Cheshire Regiment	31-12-53	13-11-48	01-12-62
6135	09-10-27	Samson	The East Lancashire Regiment	07-01-47	02-10-48	29-12-62
6136	09-10-27	Goliath	The Border Regiment	22-03-50	31-07-48	28-03-64
6137	09-10-27	Vesta	The Prince of Wales's Volunteers (South Lancashire)	16-03-55	08-05-48	03-11-62
6138	09-10-27	Fury	The London Irish Rifleman	09-06-44	15-01-49	09-02-63
6139	09-10-27	Ajax	The Welch Regiment	12-11-46	22-05-48	13-10-62
6140	09-10-27	Hector	The King's Royal Rifle Corps	30-05-52	08-01-49	30-10-65
6141	06-11-27	Caledonian	The North Staffordshire Regiment	28-10-50	03-07-48	18-04-64
6142	06-11-27	Lion	The York and Lancaster Regiment	14-02-51	03-07-48	11-01-64
6143	06-11-27	Mail	The South Staffordshire Regiment	07-06-49	04-09-48	21-12-63
6144	06-11-27	Ostrich	Honourable Artillery Company	09-06-45	05-06-48	11-01-64
6145	31-12-27	Condor	The Duke of Wellington's Regt. (West Riding)	29-01-44	02-10-48	08-12-62
6146	06-11-27	Jenny Lind	The Rifle Brigade	08-10-43	12-06-48	01-12-62
6147	06-11-27	Courier	The Northamptonshire Regiment	26-09-46	15-01-49	01-12-62
6148	04-12-27	Velocipede	The Manchester Regiment	09-07-54	26-06-48	14-11-64
6149	04-12-27	Lady of the Lake	The Middlesex Regiment	17-04-45	24-04-48	31-08-63
6150	02-06-30	The Life Guardsman		19-12-45	22-01-49	23-11-63
6151	11-06-30	The Royal Horse Guardsman		16-04-53	23-10-48	29-12-62
6152	19-06-30	The King's Dragoon Guardsman		11-08-45	19-06-48	17-04-65
6153	30-06-30	The Royal Dragoon		19-08-49	20-08-49	22-12-62
6154	07-07-30	The Hussar		16-03-48	17-04-48	01-12-62
6155	14-07-30	The Lancer		18-08-50	03-07-48	12-12-64
6156	21-07-30	The South Wales Borderer		28-05-54	05-02-49	10-10-64
6157	28-07-30	The Royal Artilleryman		19-01-46	18-12-48	04-01-64
6158	04-08-30	The Loyal Regiment		24-09-52	09-10-48	19-10-63
6159	11-08-30	The Royal Air Force		13-10-45	18-09-48	01-12-62
6160	27-08-30	Queen Victoria's Rifleman		10-02-45	25-09-48	01-05-65
6161	08-09-30	The King's Own	King's Own	12-10-46	31-07-48	01-12-62
6162	09-09-30	Queen's Westminster Rifleman		07-01-48	17-04-48	30-05-64
6163	15-09-30	Civil Service Rifleman		08-10-53	20-11-48	29-08-64
6164	22-09-30	The Artists' Rifleman		23-06-51	17-04-48	29-12-62
6165	29-09-30	The Ranger (12th London Regiment)		24-06-52	23-10-48	21-11-64
6166	06-10-30	London Rifle Brigade		10-01-45	31-07-48	19-09-64
6167	13-10-30	The Hertfordshire Regiment		13-12-48	18-12-48	11-04-64
6168	10-10-30	The Girl Guide		27-04-46	04-09-48	02-05-64
6169	27-10-30	The Boy Scout		12-05-45	15-05-48	25-05-63